Love Is Like An Orange

Poetry and Prose

Sydney Huffman

BookLeaf Publishing

India | USA | UK

Made with ❤ on the BookLeaf Publishing Platform
www.bookleafpub.in
www.bookleafpub.com

Dedication

No matter what happens, just know you are loved.

Preface

Love is Like an Orange is a poetry and prose compilation that explores themes of love and grief. Some pieces were written specifically for this collection, while others are older pieces making a resurgence.

Acknowledgements

Thank you to my brother, whose encouragement and support never wavers, even if "...Dust Bunnies hit [him] like a truck." This wouldn't have been possible without you, so thanks for always sticking by me.

Dirty Socks and Dust Bunnies

Time has frozen, and you are still smiling in the living room,
While I weave my way through scattered toys and dirty socks,
The tea kettle whistles alongside the laughs of children,
Sentient dust bunnies travel by their own volition, multiplying every second,
We always joked that *"our love was as great as our house was dirty,"*
But now our house is finally clean.

Girlhood is a Spectrum

and I am god reincarnated // and I am nothing but failure // and I am my father's worst nightmare // and I am my mother's mirror // and I'm surrounded by stupidity // and I'll never amount to anything // and I'm the happiest I've ever been // and all I do is cry // and please don't perceive me // and I want to be adored // and I can't be bothered to leave this place // and I want to be anywhere other than this house // and my youth is slipping away at an alarming rate // and adulthood can't come soon enough // and I'm an open book // and no one knows the real me // and I've never done anything wrong // and I lie awake at night haunted by my sins // and I'm the eldest daughter // and I'm literally just a girl //

There is Nothing Quite Like a Poet

"There is nothing quite like a poet," said of shaking hands frantically mashing keys and scrawling letters before those elusive words evaporated alongside creativity's muse.

"There is nothing quite like a poet," said of too many cups of coffee, one for every hour spent staring at nothing, an endless void of nothing where art was supposed to materialize.

"There is nothing quite like a poet," said of bottled-up emotions exploding like champagne over a beautiful dress, like mentos dropped into a bottle of coke, with only writing as a reprieve.

"There is nothing quite like a poet," said of elaborate daydreams, of the inherent romanticism encircling daily life, where the smallest things make the most grandiose gestures.

"There is nothing quite like a poet," said of carefully curated playlists, prompts, and Pinterest boards, each designed ~~as a procrastination technique~~ as a way to get into the writing mindset.

"There is nothing quite like a poet," said of those sitting underneath the moon, wishing on every star passing by.

"There is nothing quite like a poet," said of confessions of love and admiration, expressed through beautifully handwritten letters and whispered poetic ramblings.

"There is nothing quite like a poet," said of everlasting love, forever preserved through works of art, made to exist long after the artist is gone.

How to Make Iced Coffee

First, stand in the coffee aisle of the grocery store,
staring blankly at the different brands. Wrack your
brains to remember which brand she used to get
(something Arabic perhaps?), then just throw a bunch of
them in your cart. Maybe you'll get lucky, maybe you
won't. It's not like you can ask her which one it was.

Once home, spend 45 minutes looking for a Ball jar with
a lid that fits. Wash the dust off, fumble with the wet jar,
then clean up the broken glass and repeat the process.
Maybe take an hour or two to scream and cry and rage,
then carry on like nothing happened.

Empty coffee grounds into the jar, then add the
"pumpkin pie" spices. Allow colorful metaphors to pour
out like the spices do, until your senses are overwhelmed
by cinnamon and expletives. Next, add water until the
jar is full. Fresh, not salt, the recipe says. Yet somehow, a
few drops of saltwater find its way in there.

Screw on the lid, realize you have the wrong size, dig out
the proper one, then store the coffee in the refrigerator.
Let it steep in the cold darkness for a few hours(?),
days(?), a week(?). Time has no meaning anymore.

Strain the coffee into a cup, the blue one, not the yellow
honeycomb-shaped one. That honeycomb cup stays in
the cupboard, untouched, no longer in use, stored away
with the memories. Strain the coffee into the blue cup,
ignore the grounds that made their way in alongside the
liquid. It's not worth redoing it.

Add 3 sugars and ¼ cup of whole milk (the organic kind,
in the carton with the happy cow leaping over the
world). Lastly, try a sip and come face to face with the
crushing realization that it will never taste the same.

I Hope This Email Finds You

examining your innermost fears // thriving in spite of the horrors // using words like *cynosure*, incipient, and *mellifluous* on a daily basis // embracing the mundane // locked in a stalemate with Fate // in love with yourself // spiraling madly out of control // in a quiet field of green // at odds with your TBR pile // lost in your imagination // at ease with your skin // collecting hearts like trophies // inhaling the sweetness of success // ending on a positive note

What I Want From Love

I want a simple, steady kind of love. A waltz-through-the-mud-when-the-shit-hits-the-fan kind of love. A "play board games at 3 AM" kind of love. The kind of love made of soft morning light, soft as the fleece-lined blankets draped over the bed. A "white picket fence and friendly neighbor with cookies" kind of love. A Disney style, happily ever after kind of love. Walking hand-in-hand to the ice cream truck after dinner kind of love. The kind of love full of "*Good morning! <3*" texts and random check-ins. The kind of love that promises peaceful discussions and a warm, safe environment full of positivity. The kind of love that our children can look up to and admire. The kind of love where you'll be you, and I'll be me, and together we can simply exist.

A List of Poems I'll Never Write

1. A burden so unjustly carried

2. In medieval times I would have died by now

3. Girlhood is cherry coke and saturated lighting

4. Pretty things, carved from bones and sinew

5. "What ends the world?" you ask, blind to the luminescent steel box draining us of life

6. How to deceive a god

7. Love is a myth written into every fiber of our beings

8. It's a rainy autumn day and I am restless

9. It's 12:39am and I'm homesick again

10. I want to be scattered across a million stars

11. In the end, we are all just memories railing against
their common fate

12. The thought of your mother's crystal vase, sitting
empty in the back of a cupboard save for the dust it
collects

13. Lovely cries the heart that does not beat (for you)

14. A beautiful morning already spoiled by dream's
painted veil

15. I love you, please do not forget me

16. Maybe one day I'll get off the floor, but for now, I'll
stay here

17. Heaven was not named (but I'm pretty sure it was
you)

Lighthouse

You are like a lighthouse,
A gallant brightness cutting through the dark,
Beckoning me to my inevitable doom.

The World is Ending

and I'm putting on a smile before I go to work // and I'm asking children what they want to be when they grow up // and I'm making small talk at the dinner table // and I'm doom-scrolling through apps // and I'm hiding under a blanket so the monsters can't find me // and I'm frantically trying to live my life before it ends // and I'm blowing through my money, since it's now or never // and I'm escaping reality by any means necessary // and I'm sitting in a tiny town where nothing ever changes // and I'm about to celebrate my 21st birthday, but there's really no reason to celebrate // and I'm trying to forge relationships, but I just don't see the point // and I'm losing sleep over the way of things, but I have no power to change it // and I'm watching everything go up in flames around me // and I'm trying not to let the trolls win // and I'm telling people *"I'm fine!"* // and I'm sitting in front of my computer typing while the world is ending.

Marriage Vows

Meet me somewhere in person, where we can talk face to face for hours // I know dating apps are popular, and they are helpful, but it's easier to romanticize the sound of your voice and the way that you smile when we're together // let's exchange phone numbers and tiny gifts so that I'll always think of you when I see it // you know, I'm terrible about leaving people on read, but you never take it personally //

When we court each other, I'll bring you homemade cookies if you offer to hold my hand // the fastest way to my heart is understanding my film references and play Stardew Valley with me // in return, I'll listen to you infodump and drink bubble tea until the end of time // let's go watch off-Broadway shows then have an impromptu karaoke session on the drive back home //

Dating will feel easy, effortless, as natural as breathing //
which cliche do you think we'll fall under, the one where
we move in together on the second date, or the one
where it takes us 27 years just to hold hands? //
regardless of the length, any time spent with you is a
good time //

Propose to me onstage like that video of ballet dancers
after their final show // the one where she's en pointe,
hugging him like she'd never let go // or the one where
both girlfriends simultaneously propose at Disneyland //
or ask me in the kitchen while we're washing dishes //
either way, I'll always say yes //

We'll get married wearing ripped jeans and oversized
hoodies // with chipped nail polish and smudgy mascara
// just the two of us, no chapel, no fanfare, no
overbearing guests or crushing expenses // let's stop by
Handel's after & splurge on pricy ice cream //

Our family will be small, but I promise it'll never feel
that way // not when we're curled up on the couch
watching reruns, popcorn in hand and a kitty on lap //
we won't have children (too much parental trauma), but

that means we get to stay children forever ourselves //

15

We will only treat each other kindly, no matter how old
or grouchy we get // our love will last forever, even if our
bodies don't // bury me in the same coffin so that I'll be
with you always // or better yet, let's have our ashes
sprinkled under a tree or over a lake // it doesn't matter,
just as long as we're together //

Insanity

I have been watering dead plants for years,
Hoping that one day my insanity will pay off,
"This will be the day it changes,"
And yet,
Nothing ever does.

It is a Sin to Write

It is a sin to write about the way your name tastes on my lips in the dark of night, sweet like the honey-coated words you whisper in my ear.
It is a sin to write about the way we meld together in an embrace made of satin and lace, skin and sweat.
It is a sin to write about how your perfume brings to mind a sort of poetic lust, heady florals mixed with the warmth of vanilla and nutmeg.
It is a sin to write about the feeling of your hand in mine, like perfectly manicured puzzle pieces linked together for eternity.
It is a sin to write those three sacred words, but I trace them with my fingers along your arm, consequences be damned.
If it is a sin to write about you, then I will gladly be damned.

Thought Daughter

How to make a thought daughter:

// liquid black eyeliner & bright red lipstick // broken fingernails with garden dirt underneath // fake vintage dresses and black jeans // the ability to remember every embarrassing moment ever // classical music playlists and video game OSTs // too many cups of cold brewed coffee, drowned in milk and spices // the color purple, but only the shades in between *royal* and *plum* // cat hair on furniture, on clothes, on everything // ink-stained hands from endless lectures // overgrown gardens full of herbs and flowers // the desire to be loved, but fear of (rejection)(commitment)(falling out of love) // late nights and early mornings // always eager to please // too much sympathy for the villain // in love with every girl ever // only capable of writing poems about love and grief // dark chocolate chips at 11pm to satisfy an insatiable sweet tooth // emotionally incapable of doing laundry // the fear of turning into her parents // the inability to end poems meaningfully //

For a Moment

For a moment, I thought that I loved you.
For a moment, I thought we were different.
For a moment, I pictured our life together.
In that moment, I knew.
There would be no more moments.
And for a moment, that was okay.

Yes, I'm Drunk

Drunk on the moon, basking in all her soft glory,
Drunk on the idea of love, the way it lingers even after
everything else has faded,

Drunk on the way your skin feels against mine, like
rouge-stained
silk & Alabaster perfume,
Drunk on the tiny pleasures of life, the way cherries melt
in
one's mouth, eliciting the sweetest of sounds,

Drunk on sorrow, a grief so
profound it crushes the spirit into a bloody, ruined mess,
Drunk on the bittersweet taste
of loneliness coated in despair, with a hint of disgust on
top,

Drunk on maniac revelations, on words

pouring

                pouring

                                pouring

        on the page ~~off the page~~

Drunken thoughts reflecting the mind, ~~like the moon and
all her
soft glory~~, like the sun's burning rays, burning like a
whiskey sour,
remnants staining the page like a cloying perfume, like
blood-red lipstick
oxidizing in passion, a passion left to rot like overripe
cherries, as words
twist & spiral, morphing into screams of despair,
spiraling like the wine
at the bottom of this bottle —

I'd Write You a Letter, But...

these words taste empty as they sit on the page // just gibberish and ~~pen scratches~~ ink blots forming an unknown language // met with frustration // writer's block is a disease claiming time is the cure // freewriting is a hell unlike any other // the words dissipate like bubbles, popping merrily as time laughs and continues on // five minutes is an eternity when staring at a blank page // distractions glow brighter than the blaringly harsh white of paper untouched // and suddenly it's a brilliant idea to write a letter

In Another Life, Maybe We're Soulmates

Maybe our love was as easy as breathing,
Or maybe it didn't exist at all.
Fate could have taken pity on us,
But instead, here we are.

How To Write a Poem

Step 1: Stare at the blank white void known as "paper" until words have completely dissipated from your mind and your eyes have started to bleed.

Step 2: Pour over books from dozens of poets, spanning hundreds of years to just a few; lose yourself down the IG poetry rabbit hole, with the beautiful quotes edited onto stunningly aesthetic backgrounds; attend live poetry readings so that your mind can wander and mull over the author's intentions.

Step 3: Throw yourself heart first into tragic situations, letting grief wash over you like a devastating hurricane; find solace in the moon, a piece of shared fruit, the thousand ways humans say "I love you," the comforting touch of a loved one.

Step 4: Pour your fucking soul out onto that piece of paper, until there's no room to possibly write any more, then continue in the margins. Write freely, without a care in the world, until the early hours of the morning, & when you're satisfied with how it feels, allow the ink to dry while you take a much-deserved rest.

Step 5: Reread what you wrote, then erase it. After all, it'll never be as good as a real poet's work.

Revelations

There's a god in my house,

He toys with matches like a lover's caress, as quick to create as he is to destroy.

I tell him about the time I was thirteen and discovered self-loathing, the way it lingered in my mouth like old pennies and razor blades. I tell him how even now, the shame drips down my body, pooling at my feet. The smell is suffocating, like gasoline.

He offers me a lighter, as well as a sewing kit. *To fix the world, or burn it down.* He doesn't know the answer yet, and frankly neither do I.

There's a siren in my bed,

She sings of love and lust and madness, the gentle kind that latches on when it's too late to be stopped.

I tell her about the girl I kissed at nineteen, with her golden hair and bruised knuckles. I tell her about the way my hands shook when I worshipped her, the way the bruises faded off her hands and into my heart.

She hums in time with the rustle of the fleecy comforter, the sensation soothing and stilling until only her loving promises remain. *Bruises will fade, feelings will not.* One day I will learn to live with that.

There's a faerie in my garden,

He sits amongst the weeping roses, mindlessly weaving flower crowns for an aching empire.

I tell him stories of my youth, where small children led big lives full of adventure and mischief. I tell him how those lives shrank as we grew older, until one day they simply ceased to exist entirely.

He kisses the words, the taste of tangerine and honeysuckle a sweet stain on each memory. *A bitter yet unavoidable fate, like summer's passing.* Innocence slips through thorn-pricked hands, mixing with the blood and earth beneath my feet.

There's an angel in my bathroom,

They scrawl inspirational messages in sharpie on the
paper dispenser, despites tears streaming from a
thousand eyes.

I tell them about my twenty-first birthday, where each
drink swallowed had oxidized in my bloodstream until
all I could do was lay down and weep. I tell them how
only the note written in pink lipstick on the grimy
bathroom mirror kept me sane. *"YOU ARE LOVED <3"*

They wrap their wings around me, as though to shield
from the storm inside and whisper *"you are loved, you
are loved, you are loved."* Perhaps one day I'll believe it.

Living is an Act of Desperation

and I will cling to this life with everything I've got // and I will succeed even if it kills me // and I will prove my father wrong // and I will remain gentle and kind // and I will make a name for myself // and I will be happy one day // and I will be a force to be reckoned with // and I will live my life to the fullest // and I will conquer fate // and I will be the better person // and I will surround myself with love / /and I will keep on trying // and I will yield to no man // and I will find joy in the mundane // and I will write, sing, and dance like there's no tomorrow // and I will make my dreams a reality // and I will hope for a better future // and I will figure it out // and I will hold my younger self tightly // and I will learn to temper my grief // and I will live as though there's nothing else for me to do.

Love is Like an Orange

Love is like an orange, I muse as I watch her cast aside her orange peels, letting them fall to the road without a care in the world. *Some treasure it in its entire form, while others tear into it until they get what they want.*

Love is like an orange. I bite into the fruit & reflect on its taste. In this moment here, with tingling tastebuds & sticky fingers, nothing else seems to matter. *Sweet, vibrant, & full of life.*

Love is like an orange, I think to myself as I offer up slices of orange alongside my heart. *Meant to be broken into pieces, meant to be given to those around you.*

Love is like an orange. She's gone now, & in this moment I feel like one of her orange peels, discarded, no longer of use. *Sour, unpleasant, shriveling away to rot.*

Love is like an orange. My best friend slices an orange in half, scoops out the insides & fills them with oil, then sets the stem ablaze. It feels like a reflection of my heart. *Bright & fiery, a comforting warmth or painful burns.*

Love is like an orange. I reflect on my sister's tendency to plant each & every orange seed, to compost the peels so that no part goes unused. *While one part may seem more appealing, we shouldn't neglect one for the other. The same goes for love.*

Love is like an orange. The delicate scent of orange blossoms fills my nose & reminds me that citrus season is coming. *Fragile & fleeting, yet purely irresistible.*

Love is like an orange. When orange season arrives, my grandmother makes dozens of treats, from candied slices to marmalades to citrus wheels to juice. *There are no limits to what you can make with oranges, or with love.*

Love is like an orange. You laugh as you fumble with an orange, the fruit bursting between your fingers before you're able to eat it. I could listen to that laugh forever. *My heart feels like it could burst open, much like a juicy orange, just from being here with you.*

I smile at the basket of oranges on the porch, with a note that says,
"Love is like an orange. It reminds me of you."

www.ingramcontent.com/pod-product-compliance
Lightning Source LLC
LaVergne TN
LVHW010022200726